Get your Sh*t Together Planner

KATE GROSVENOR

Copyright © 2021 by Kate Grosvenor

All rights reserved. This book or any portion thereof may not be reproduced or used in any manner whatsoever without the express written permission of the publisher except for the use of brief quotations in a book review or scholarly journal.

First Printing: 2021

Kate Grosvenor Coaching Limited
Epic House, 18 Darnall Road
Sheffield, South Yorkshire. S9 5AB
United Kingdom
www.kategrosvenor.com

About the Creator

Kate Grosvenor lives in Yorkshire with her partner, three daughters, four cats, and three horses.

She is a Transformational Life Coach, former Headteacher with a background in Psychology, and is a best-selling author of psychology and lifestyle books, planners and journals.

Despite having a master's degree, a bachelor's degree, diplomas and more, Kate believes that the letters after her name are not the secret to her coaching success.

What matters is that she understands how you feel and has experienced so many heartaches in life – from growing up with an alcoholic mother, to being a survivor of domestic violence and overcoming near-bankruptcy, life-threatening obesity, addiction to prescription sleeping pills, antidepressants, painkillers and more.

She coaches from a place of "I get how this feels, let me teach you how to make it so much better." Kate, herself, is a self-confessed gratitude junkie, journal queen, and leads what she describes as an unbelievably joyous and beautiful life.

Kate is a regular contributor on BBC Radio Leeds & BBC Radio Sheffield and has been on both local and national BBC Radio, as well being regularly featured as a writer in several magazines. In 2020 she became an Honouree of the ATHENA International SCR Leadership Award and was nominated for Business of the Year too.

For Kate's Feed Your Fairy Membership, Signature Transformation Programme, 1-2-1 coaching, and more, pop to her website. Follow her on social media for coaching videos, advice, tips, and more.

FOR A TRAINING VIDEO ON HOW TO USE THIS PLANNER, OR OTHER EMPOWERED WOMAN PLANNERS PLEASE GO TO **WWW.EMPOWEREDWOMANPLANNERS.COM**.

WWW.KATEGROSVENOR.COM

MONTH
01

GOOD ORGANISING IS NOT ABOUT CHANGING YOUR PERSONALITY.

JUST YOUR HABITS.

WWW.KATEGROSVENOR.COM

My Month at a Glance

Notes:

Goal Setting
Reflecting and Looking Ahead

Top Moments ★	Most Proud of ★	Promises to Make Myself ★

Personal Goals	9-5 Goals	Health Goals

I will Try to Stop	I would Like To Learn	Habits I want to Adopt

People I want to Connect with	I want to Save	I want to Buy

Goal Tracker

Pick Your Top 3 Goals for This Month

GOAL: _____

START DATE: _____

DEADLINE: _____

Break down goals into daily action steps. Track progress below.

Date	Task	Description	Deadline	Status

Monthly Project Planning

Reflection

What was working	What was not working

Get Busy & Source

Project To-Do List	Project Supply List

Schedule it!

Sunday	Monday	Tuesday	Wednesday	Thursday	Friday	Saturday

Monthly Expenses

Recurring Expenses

Memberships, etc.	Amount
TOTAL RECURRING EXPENSES	£

Variable Expenses

	Amount
TOTAL VARIABLE EXPENSES	£
TOTAL MONTHLY EXPENSES	£

Monthly Cleaning Plan

Sunday	Monday	Tuesday	Wednesday	Thursday	Friday	Saturday	Sunday

Daily
-
-
-
-

Weekly
-
-
-
-

Monthly
-
-
-
-

Monthly Decluttering Plan

KITCHEN

- ✓ Empty boxes of food
- ✓ Expired food
- ✓ Chipped/cracked dishes, plates, etc.
- ✓ Bent cutlery
- ✓ Rusty/dull knives
- ✓ Stained/broken/worn kitchen utensils
- ✓ Tidy plastic bags, ties, and clips
- ✓ Sort Tupperware - bin any with missing lids
- ✓ Bin and pans with cracked/peeling non-stick
- ✓ Clean and fill condiment jars/spices
- ✓ Wash oven gloves, etc. and restock cloths
- ✓ Consolidate all cleaning products
- ✓ Wash and sanitise kitchen bin

BEDROOM

- ✓ Clean dressing table
- ✓ Wash make up brushes
- ✓ Bin any out-of-date/broken make up
- ✓ Remove old magazines/old books
- ✓ Clean shoes & bags and stuff with tissue paper
- ✓ Sell/send to charity shop any clothes that don't fit
- ✓ Recycle any torn clothes
- ✓ Remove any clothes out of season and store
- ✓ Sort socks. Bin any without pairs
- ✓ Bin any torn/stretched underwear
- ✓ Sort drawers and arrange according to use/colour

BATHROOM

- ✓ Clean under sink
- ✓ Bin old toothbrush/es
- ✓ Empty shampoo/conditioner
- ✓ Bin stretched hair ties
- ✓ Remove any tatty faceclothes/towels
- ✓ Throw away empty toiletries
- ✓ Bin dried up nail polish
- ✓ Restock cotton wool pads & buds
- ✓ Check sanitary products and consolidate
- ✓ Refill liquid soap

LAUNDRY

- ✓ Empty lint from tumble dryer
- ✓ Wash out detergent drawer
- ✓ Clean/sanitise washing machine
- ✓ Refil detergent/softener containers

CLEANING

- ✓ Recycle broken spray bottles
- ✓ Clean under sink and sanitise
- ✓ Consolidate all cleaning products
- ✓ Store excess brushes or sponges

NOTES

Notes

WEEK 01

"I REGRET FEELING ORGANISED"

(SAID NO WOMAN EVER)

WWW.KATEGROSVENOR.COM

W/C ....

My Week's Appointments

Monday

Tuesday

Wednesday

Thursday

Friday

Saturday

Sunday

Notes:

MASTER TA-DA! LIST

Write down everything that NEEDS to get done this week.

....
....
....
....
....
....
....
....
....
....
....
....
....
....
....
....
....
....
....
....
....
....
....
....
....
....
....
....
....
....
....
....
....

Now, cross out everything off this list that doesn't belong to YOU. This is YOUR ta-da! list and is for YOUR important things this week.

DAILY TA-DA'S!

Write 4 things in each day, no more.

MONDAY
- ☐ ....
- ☐ ....
- ☐ ....
- ☐ ....

TUESDAY
- ☐ ....
- ☐ ....
- ☐ ....
- ☐ ....

WEDNESDAY
- ☐ ....
- ☐ ....
- ☐ ....
- ☐ ....

THURSDAY
- ☐ ....
- ☐ ....
- ☐ ....
- ☐ ....

FRIDAY
- ☐ ....
- ☐ ....
- ☐ ....
- ☐ ....

SATURDAY
- ☐ ....
- ☐ ....
- ☐ ....
- ☐ ....

SUNDAY
- ☐ ....
- ☐ ....
- ☐ ....
- ☐ ....

SOMETIME THIS WEEK
- ☐ ....
- ☐ ....
- ☐ ....
- ☐ ....

WEEKLY MEAL PLANNER

SUNDAY

SATURDAY

FRIDAY

THURSDAY

WEDNESDAY

TUESDAY

MONDAY

Shopping List

Notes

WEEKLY FITNESS PLANNER

PROGRESS & FOCUS

SUNDAY

SATURDAY

FRIDAY

THURSDAY

WEDNESDAY

TUESDAY

MONDAY

NOTES

DATE ....

DAILY PLANNER

DAILY TA-DA'S

1.
2.
3.

CHECK LIST

- _____
- _____
- _____
- _____
- _____
- _____
- _____
- _____
- _____
- _____

SCHEDULE

:	
:	
:	
:	
:	
:	
:	
:	
:	
:	

FUTURE TASKS

→
→
→
→

TRACKER

(?)(?)(?)(?)(?)(?)(?)(?)(?)(?)
(?)(?)(?)(?)(?)(?)(?)(?)(?)(?)

DATE ....

Daily Planner

Daily Ta-Da's

1.
2.
3.

Check List

- _____
- _____
- _____
- _____
- _____
- _____
- _____
- _____
- _____
- _____

Schedule

:	
:	
:	
:	
:	
:	
:	
:	
:	
:	

Future Tasks

→
→
→
→

Tracker

DATE ....

Daily Planner

Daily Ta-Da's

1.
2.
3.

Check List

- _____
- _____
- _____
- _____
- _____
- _____
- _____
- _____
- _____
- _____

Schedule

:	
:	
:	
:	
:	
:	
:	
:	
:	
:	

Future Tasks

→ _____
→ _____
→ _____
→ _____

Tracker

? ? ? ? ? ? ? ? ? ?
? ? ? ? ? ? ? ? ? ?

DATE ....

Daily Planner

Daily Ta-Da's

1.
2.
3.

Check List

- _____
- _____
- _____
- _____
- _____
- _____
- _____
- _____
- _____

Schedule

:	
:	
:	
:	
:	
:	
:	
:	
:	
:	

Future Tasks

→
→
→
→

Tracker

DATE ....

Daily Planner

Daily Ta-Da's

1.
2.
3.

Check List

- _____
- _____
- _____
- _____
- _____
- _____
- _____
- _____
- _____
- _____

Schedule

:	
:	
:	
:	
:	
:	
:	
:	
:	
:	

Future Tasks

→
→
→
→

Tracker

(?)(?)(?)(?)(?)(?)(?)(?)(?)(?)
(?)(?)(?)(?)(?)(?)(?)(?)(?)(?)

DATE ....

DAILY PLANNER

DAILY TA-DA'S

1.
2.
3.

CHECK LIST

- _____
- _____
- _____
- _____
- _____
- _____
- _____
- _____
- _____
- _____

SCHEDULE

:	
:	
:	
:	
:	
:	
:	
:	
:	
:	

FUTURE TASKS

→
→
→
→

TRACKER

? ? ? ? ? ? ? ? ? ?
? ? ? ? ? ? ? ? ? ?

DATE ....

DAILY PLANNER

DAILY TA-DA'S

1.
2.
3.

CHECK LIST

- _____
- _____
- _____
- _____
- _____
- _____
- _____
- _____
- _____
- _____

SCHEDULE

:	
:	
:	
:	
:	
:	
:	
:	
:	
:	

FUTURE TASKS

→
→
→
→

TRACKER

Sunday Review

On reflection, how did this week go?

What achievements am I proud of this week?

Who is the woman I need to become to achieve my goals?

Little promises I'm making to myself for next week

Notes

Notes

WEEK 02

ALL TOO OFTEN WE GET STUCK ON THE FACT THAT BEING ORGANISED MEANS BEING PERFECT ABOUT EVERYTHING.

NOT TRUE. IT JUST NEEDS TO "FEEL" GOOD TO YOU.

WWW.KATEGROSVENOR.COM

W/C ....

My Week's Appointments

Monday	Tuesday	Wednesday

Thursday	Friday	Saturday
		Sunday

Notes:

MASTER TA-DA! LIST

Write down everything that NEEDS to get done this week.

....
....
....
....
....
....
....
....
....
....
....
....
....
....
....
....
....
....
....
....
....
....
....
....
....
....
....
....
....
....
....
....

Now, cross out everything off this list that doesn't belong to YOU. This is YOUR ta-da! list and is for YOUR important things this week.

DAILY TA-DA'S!

Write 4 things in each day, no more.

MONDAY	TUESDAY
☐	☐ ....
☐	☐ ....
☐	☐ ....
☐	☐ ....

WEDNESDAY	THURSDAY
☐	☐ ....
☐	☐ ....
☐	☐ ....
☐	☐ ....

FRIDAY	SATURDAY
☐	☐ ....
☐	☐ ....
☐	☐ ....
☐	☐ ....

SUNDAY	SOMETIME THIS WEEK
☐	☐ ....
☐	☐ ....
☐	☐ ....
☐	☐ ....

WEEKLY MEAL PLANNER

SUNDAY

SATURDAY

FRIDAY

THURSDAY

WEDNESDAY

TUESDAY

MONDAY

Shopping List

Notes

WEEKLY FITNESS PLANNER

SUNDAY	
SATURDAY	
FRIDAY	
THURSDAY	
WEDNESDAY	
TUESDAY	
MONDAY	

Progress & Focus

Notes

DATE ....

Daily Planner

Daily Ta-Da's

1.
2.
3.

Check List

-
-
-
-
-
-
-
-
-
-

Schedule

:	
:	
:	
:	
:	
:	
:	
:	
:	
:	

Future Tasks

→
→
→
→

Tracker

(?)(?)(?)(?)(?)(?)(?)(?)(?)(?)
(?)(?)(?)(?)(?)(?)(?)(?)(?)(?)

Date ....

Daily Planner

Daily Ta-Da's

1.
2.
3.

Check List

-
-
-
-
-
-
-
-
-

Schedule

:	
:	
:	
:	
:	
:	
:	
:	
:	
:	

Future Tasks

→
→
→
→

Tracker

DATE ....

Daily Planner

Daily Ta-Da's

1.
2.
3.

Check List

- [ ]
- [ ]
- [ ]
- [ ]
- [ ]
- [ ]
- [ ]
- [ ]
- [ ]
- [ ]

Schedule

:	
:	
:	
:	
:	
:	
:	
:	
:	
:	

Future Tasks

→
→
→
→

Tracker

Date ....

Daily Planner

Daily Ta-Da's

1.
2.
3.

Check List

- ☑ _____
- ☑ _____
- ☑ _____
- ☑ _____
- ☑ _____
- ☑ _____
- ☑ _____
- ☑ _____
- ☑ _____
- ☑ _____

Schedule

:	
:	
:	
:	
:	
:	
:	
:	
:	
:	

Future Tasks

→
→
→
→

Tracker

? ? ? ? ? ? ? ? ? ?
? ? ? ? ? ? ? ? ? ?

DATE ....

Daily Planner

Daily Ta-Da's

1.
2.
3.

Check List

- _____
- _____
- _____
- _____
- _____
- _____
- _____
- _____
- _____
- _____

Schedule

:	
:	
:	
:	
:	
:	
:	
:	
:	
:	

Future Tasks

→
→
→
→

Tracker

? ? ? ? ? ? ? ? ? ?
? ? ? ? ? ? ? ? ? ?

Date ....

Daily Planner

Daily Ta-Da's

1.
2.
3.

Check List

-
-
-
-
-
-
-
-
-
-

Schedule

:	
:	
:	
:	
:	
:	
:	
:	
:	
:	

Future Tasks

→
→
→
→

Tracker

? ? ? ? ? ? ? ? ? ?
? ? ? ? ? ? ? ? ? ?

Date ....

Daily Planner

Daily Ta-Da's

1.
2.
3.

Check List

-
-
-
-
-
-
-
-
-
-

Schedule

:	
:	
:	
:	
:	
:	
:	
:	
:	
:	

Future Tasks

→
→
→
→

Tracker

? ? ? ? ? ? ? ? ? ?
? ? ? ? ? ? ? ? ? ?

Sunday Review

On reflection, how did this week go?

What achievements am I proud of this week?

Who is the woman I need to become to achieve my goals?

Little promises I'm making to myself for next week

Notes

NOTES

WEEK 03

FEELING ORGANISED IS ABOUT
TWO THINGS:

KEEPING WHAT YOU NEED, WHICH
ADDS VALUE, & BRINGS YOU JOY.

GETTING RID OF THE REST.

WWW.KATEGROSVENOR.COM

W/C ....

My Week's Appointments

Monday	Tuesday	Wednesday

Thursday	Friday	Saturday
		Sunday

Notes:

MASTER TA-DA! LIST

WRITE DOWN EVERYTHING THAT NEEDS TO GET DONE THIS WEEK.

NOW, CROSS OUT EVERYTHING OFF THIS LIST THAT DOESN'T BELONG TO YOU.
THIS IS YOUR TA-DA! LIST AND IS FOR YOUR IMPORTANT THINGS THIS WEEK.

DAILY TA-DA'S!

Write 4 things in each day, no more.

MONDAY
- ☐ ....
- ☐ ....
- ☐ ....
- ☐ ....

TUESDAY
- ☐ ....
- ☐ ....
- ☐ ....
- ☐ ....

WEDNESDAY
- ☐ ....
- ☐ ....
- ☐ ....
- ☐ ....

THURSDAY
- ☐ ....
- ☐ ....
- ☐ ....
- ☐ ....

FRIDAY
- ☐ ....
- ☐ ....
- ☐ ....
- ☐ ....

SATURDAY
- ☐ ....
- ☐ ....
- ☐ ....
- ☐ ....

SUNDAY
- ☐ ....
- ☐ ....
- ☐ ....
- ☐ ....

SOMETIME THIS WEEK
- ☐ ....
- ☐ ....
- ☐ ....
- ☐ ....

WEEKLY MEAL PLANNER

SUNDAY

SATURDAY

FRIDAY

THURSDAY

WEDNESDAY

TUESDAY

MONDAY

Shopping List

Notes

WEEKLY FITNESS PLANNER

SUNDAY	
SATURDAY	
FRIDAY	
THURSDAY	
WEDNESDAY	
TUESDAY	
MONDAY	

Progress & Focus

Notes

DATE ....

Daily Planner

Daily Ta-Da's

1.
2.
3.

Check List

-
-
-
-
-
-
-
-
-
-

Schedule

:	
:	
:	
:	
:	
:	
:	
:	
:	
:	

Future Tasks

→
→
→
→

Tracker

DATE ....

DAILY PLANNER

DAILY TA-DA'S

1.
2.
3.

CHECK LIST

- _____
- _____
- _____
- _____
- _____
- _____
- _____
- _____
- _____
- _____

SCHEDULE

:	
:	
:	
:	
:	
:	
:	
:	
:	
:	

FUTURE TASKS

→
→
→
→

TRACKER

(?)(?)(?)(?)(?)(?)(?)(?)(?)(?)
(?)(?)(?)(?)(?)(?)(?)(?)(?)(?)

Date ....

Daily Planner

Daily Ta-Da's

1.
2.
3.

Check List

- [ ]
- [ ]
- [ ]
- [ ]
- [ ]
- [ ]
- [ ]
- [ ]
- [ ]
- [ ]

Schedule

:	
:	
:	
:	
:	
:	
:	
:	
:	
:	

Future Tasks

→
→
→
→

Tracker

DATE ....

Daily Planner

Daily Ta-Da's

1.
2.
3.

Check List

- [ ] _____
- [ ] _____
- [ ] _____
- [ ] _____
- [ ] _____
- [ ] _____
- [ ] _____
- [ ] _____
- [ ] _____
- [ ] _____

Schedule

:	
:	
:	
:	
:	
:	
:	
:	
:	
:	

Future Tasks

→
→
→
→

Tracker

? ? ? ? ? ? ? ? ? ?
? ? ? ? ? ? ? ? ? ?

Date ....

Daily Planner

Daily Ta-Da's

1.
2.
3.

Check List

Schedule

:	
:	
:	
:	
:	
:	
:	
:	
:	
:	

Future Tasks

→
→
→
→

Tracker

Date ....

Daily Planner

Daily Ta-Da's

1.
2.
3.

Check List

Schedule

Future Tasks

Tracker

Date ....

Daily Planner

Daily Ta-Da's

1.
2.
3.

Check List

- _____
- _____
- _____
- _____
- _____
- _____
- _____
- _____
- _____
- _____

Schedule

:	
:	
:	
:	
:	
:	
:	
:	
:	
:	

Future Tasks

→
→
→
→

Tracker

Sunday Review

On reflection, how did this week go?

_____
_____
_____
_____
_____
_____

What achievements am I proud of this week?

_____
_____
_____
_____
_____
_____

Who is the woman I need to become to achieve my goals?

_____
_____
_____
_____
_____
_____

Little promises I'm making to myself for next week

_____
_____
_____
_____
_____
_____

NOTES

Notes

WEEK 04

ORGANISE YOUR LIFE AROUND YOUR GOALS AND WATCH YOU SMASH THEM!

WWW.KATEGROSVENOR.COM

W/C ....

My Week's Appointments

Monday	Tuesday	Wednesday

Thursday	Friday	Saturday

Sunday

Notes:

MASTER TA-DA! LIST

Write down everything that NEEDS to get done this week.

....
....
....
....
....
....
....
....
....
....
....
....
....
....
....
....
....
....
....
....
....
....
....
....
....
....
....
....
....
....

Now, cross out everything off this list that doesn't belong to YOU.
This is YOUR ta-da! list and is for YOUR important things this week.

DAILY TA-DA'S!

Write 4 things in each day, no more.

MONDAY
- ☐ ....
- ☐ ....
- ☐ ....
- ☐ ....

TUESDAY
- ☐ ....
- ☐ ....
- ☐ ....
- ☐ ....

WEDNESDAY
- ☐ ....
- ☐ ....
- ☐ ....
- ☐ ....

THURSDAY
- ☐ ....
- ☐ ....
- ☐ ....
- ☐ ....

FRIDAY
- ☐ ....
- ☐ ....
- ☐ ....
- ☐ ....

SATURDAY
- ☐ ....
- ☐ ....
- ☐ ....
- ☐ ....

SUNDAY
- ☐ ....
- ☐ ....
- ☐ ....
- ☐ ....

SOMETIME THIS WEEK
- ☐ ....
- ☐ ....
- ☐ ....
- ☐ ....

WEEKLY MEAL PLANNER

SUNDAY	
SATURDAY	
FRIDAY	
THURSDAY	
WEDNESDAY	
TUESDAY	
MONDAY	

Shopping List

Notes

WEEKLY FITNESS PLANNER

Progress & Focus

SUNDAY	
SATURDAY	
FRIDAY	
THURSDAY	
WEDNESDAY	
TUESDAY	
MONDAY	

Notes

DATE ....

Daily Planner

Daily Ta-Da's

1.
2.
3.

Check List

- _____
- _____
- _____
- _____
- _____
- _____
- _____
- _____
- _____
- _____

Schedule

:	
:	
:	
:	
:	
:	
:	
:	
:	
:	

Future Tasks

→
→
→
→

Tracker

DATE ....

DAILY PLANNER

DAILY TA-DA'S

1.
2.
3.

CHECK LIST

-
-
-
-
-
-
-
-
-

SCHEDULE

:	
:	
:	
:	
:	
:	
:	
:	
:	
:	

FUTURE TASKS

→
→
→
→

TRACKER

(?)(?)(?)(?)(?)(?)(?)(?)(?)(?)(?)
(?)(?)(?)(?)(?)(?)(?)(?)(?)(?)(?)

Date ....

Daily Planner

Daily Ta-Da's

1.
2.
3.

Check List

-
-
-
-
-
-
-
-
-
-

Schedule

:	
:	
:	
:	
:	
:	
:	
:	
:	
:	

Future Tasks

→
→
→
→

Tracker

DATE ....

DAILY PLANNER

DAILY TA-DA'S

1.
2.
3.

CHECK LIST

- _____
- _____
- _____
- _____
- _____
- _____
- _____
- _____
- _____
- _____

SCHEDULE

:	
:	
:	
:	
:	
:	
:	
:	
:	
:	

FUTURE TASKS

→
→
→
→

TRACKER

(?)(?)(?)(?)(?)(?)(?)(?)(?)(?)
(?)(?)(?)(?)(?)(?)(?)(?)(?)(?)

DATE ....

Daily Planner

Daily Ta-Da's

1.
2.
3.

Check List

- ☑ _____
- ☑ _____
- ☑ _____
- ☑ _____
- ☑ _____
- ☑ _____
- ☑ _____
- ☑ _____
- ☑ _____
- ☑ _____

Schedule

:	
:	
:	
:	
:	
:	
:	
:	
:	
:	

Future Tasks

→
→
→
→

Tracker

? ? ? ? ? ? ? ? ? ?
? ? ? ? ? ? ? ? ? ?

DATE ....

DAILY PLANNER

DAILY TA-DA'S

1.
2.
3.

CHECK LIST

- _____
- _____
- _____
- _____
- _____
- _____
- _____
- _____
- _____

SCHEDULE

:	
:	
:	
:	
:	
:	
:	
:	
:	
:	

FUTURE TASKS

→
→
→
→

TRACKER

(?)(?)(?)(?)(?)(?)(?)(?)(?)(?)
(?)(?)(?)(?)(?)(?)(?)(?)(?)(?)

DATE ....

Daily Planner

Daily Ta-Da's

1.
2.
3.

Check List

-
-
-
-
-
-
-
-
-

Schedule

:	
:	
:	
:	
:	
:	
:	
:	
:	
:	

Future Tasks

→
→
→
→

Tracker

Sunday Review

On reflection, how did this week go?

What achievements am I proud of this week?

Who is the woman I need to become to achieve my goals?

Little promises I'm making to myself for next week

Notes

Notes

Month

02

MAKE DECISIONS ABOUT WHAT **NOT** TO DO (AS WELL AS WHAT TO DO MORE OF) AND LIFE WILL FEEL SO MUCH BETTER.

WWW.KATEGROSVENOR.COM

My Month at a Glance

NOTES:

Goal Setting
REFLECTING AND LOOKING AHEAD

Top Moments ★	Most Proud of ★	Promises to Make Myself ★

Personal Goals ◎	9-5 Goals 💡	Health Goals 💓

I will Try to Stop 🚫	I would Like To Learn 👓	Habits I want to Adopt

People I want to Connect with 👤	I want to Save 🐖	I want to Buy 🛒

Goal Tracker
Pick Your Top 3 Goals for this Month

Goal: _____

Start Date: _____

Deadline: _____

Break down goals into daily action steps.
Track progress below.

Date	Task	Description	Deadline	Status

Monthly Project Planning

Reflection

What was working	What was not working

Get Busy & Source

Project To-Do List	Project Supply List

Schedule it!

Sunday	Monday	Tuesday	Wednesday	Thursday	Friday	Saturday

Monthly Expenses

RECURRING EXPENSES

Memberships, etc.	Amount
TOTAL RECURRING EXPENSES	£

VARIABLE EXPENSES

	Amount
TOTAL VARIABLE EXPENSES	£
TOTAL MONTHLY EXPENSES	£

Monthly Cleaning Plan

Sunday	Monday	Tuesday	Wednesday	Thursday	Friday	Saturday	Sunday

Daily
- [ ]
- [ ]
- [ ]
- [ ]

Weekly
- [ ]
- [ ]
- [ ]
- [ ]

Monthly
- [ ]
- [ ]
- [ ]
- [ ]

Monthly Decluttering Plan

KITCHEN

- Empty boxes of food
- Expired food
- Chipped/cracked dishes, plates, etc.
- Bent cutlery
- Rusty/dull knives
- Stained/broken/worn kitchen utensils
- Tidy plastic bags, ties, and clips
- Sort Tupperware - bin any with missing lids
- Bin and pans with cracked/peeling non-stick
- Clean and fill condiment jars/spices
- Wash oven gloves, etc. and restock cloths
- Consolidate all cleaning products
- Wash and sanitise kitchen bin

BEDROOM

- Clean dressing table
- Wash make up brushes
- Bin any out-of-date/broken make up
- Remove old magazines/old books
- Clean shoes & bags and stuff with tissue paper
- Sell/send to charity shop any clothes that don't fit
- Recycle any torn clothes
- Remove any clothes out of season and store
- Sort socks. Bin any without pairs
- Bin any torn/stretched underwear
- Sort drawers and arrange according to use/colour

BATHROOM

- Clean under sink
- Bin old toothbrush/es
- Empty shampoo/conditioner
- Bin stretched hair ties
- Remove any tatty faceclothes/towels
- Throw away empty toiletries
- Bin dried up nail polish
- Restock cotton wool pads & buds
- Check sanitary products and consolidate
- Refill liquid soap

LAUNDRY

- Empty lint from tumble dryer
- Wash out detergent drawer
- Clean/sanitise washing machine
- Refil detergent/softener containers

CLEANING

- Recycle broken spray bottles
- Clean under sink and sanitise
- Consolidate all cleaning products
- Store excess brushes or sponges

Notes

Notes

WEEK 01

THE TRUTH IS THAT FEELING
ORGANISED BRINGS
PEACE & CALMNESS

(GOOD FOR THE SOUL)

WWW.KATEGROSVENOR.COM

W/C ....

My Week's Appointments

Monday	Tuesday	Wednesday

Thursday	Friday	Saturday
		Sunday

Notes:

MASTER TA-DA! LIST

WRITE DOWN EVERYTHING THAT NEEDS TO GET DONE THIS WEEK.

....
....
....
....
....
....
....
....
....
....
....
....
....
....
....
....
....
....
....
....
....
....
....
....
....
....
....
....
....
....
....
....
....

NOW, CROSS OUT EVERYTHING OFF THIS LIST THAT DOESN'T BELONG TO YOU.
THIS IS YOUR TA-DA! LIST AND IS FOR YOUR IMPORTANT THINGS THIS WEEK.

DAILY TA-DA'S!

Write 4 things in each day, no more.

MONDAY
- ☐ ....
- ☐ ....
- ☐ ....
- ☐ ....

TUESDAY
- ☐ ....
- ☐ ....
- ☐ ....
- ☐ ....

WEDNESDAY
- ☐ ....
- ☐ ....
- ☐ ....
- ☐ ....

THURSDAY
- ☐ ....
- ☐ ....
- ☐ ....
- ☐ ....

FRIDAY
- ☐ ....
- ☐ ....
- ☐ ....
- ☐ ....

SATURDAY
- ☐ ....
- ☐ ....
- ☐ ....
- ☐ ....

SUNDAY
- ☐ ....
- ☐ ....
- ☐ ....
- ☐ ....

SOMETIME THIS WEEK
- ☐ ....
- ☐ ....
- ☐ ....
- ☐ ....

WEEKLY MEAL PLANNER

SUNDAY	
SATURDAY	
FRIDAY	
THURSDAY	
WEDNESDAY	
TUESDAY	
MONDAY	

Shopping List

Notes

WEEKLY FITNESS PLANNER

	PROGRESS & FOCUS
SUNDAY	
SATURDAY	
FRIDAY	
THURSDAY	
WEDNESDAY	
TUESDAY	
MONDAY	

NOTES

DATE ....

DAILY PLANNER

DAILY TA-DA'S

1.
2.
3.

CHECK LIST

- ☑ _____
- ☑ _____
- ☑ _____
- ☑ _____
- ☑ _____
- ☑ _____
- ☑ _____
- ☑ _____
- ☑ _____
- ☑ _____

SCHEDULE

:	
:	
:	
:	
:	
:	
:	
:	
:	
:	

FUTURE TASKS

→
→
→
→

TRACKER

? ? ? ? ? ? ? ? ? ?
? ? ? ? ? ? ? ? ? ?

DATE ....

Daily Planner

Daily Ta-Da's

1.
2.
3.

Check List

- ☑ _____
- ☑ _____
- ☑ _____
- ☑ _____
- ☑ _____
- ☑ _____
- ☑ _____
- ☑ _____
- ☑ _____
- ☑ _____

Schedule

:	
:	
:	
:	
:	
:	
:	
:	
:	
:	

Future Tasks

→
→
→
→

Tracker

? ? ? ? ? ? ? ? ? ?
? ? ? ? ? ? ? ? ? ?

DATE ....

Daily Planner

Daily Ta-Da's

1.
2.
3.

Check List

-
-
-
-
-
-
-
-
-
-

Schedule

:	
:	
:	
:	
:	
:	
:	
:	
:	
:	

Future Tasks

→
→
→
→

Tracker

(?)(?)(?)(?)(?)(?)(?)(?)(?)(?)
(?)(?)(?)(?)(?)(?)(?)(?)(?)(?)

DATE ....

DAILY PLANNER

DAILY TA-DA'S

1.
2.
3.

CHECK LIST

-
-
-
-
-
-
-
-
-

SCHEDULE

:	
:	
:	
:	
:	
:	
:	
:	
:	
:	

FUTURE TASKS

→
→
→
→

TRACKER

(?)(?)(?)(?)(?)(?)(?)(?)(?)(?)
(?)(?)(?)(?)(?)(?)(?)(?)(?)(?)

DATE ....

Daily Planner

Daily Ta-Da's

1.
2.
3.

Check List

- _____
- _____
- _____
- _____
- _____
- _____
- _____
- _____
- _____
- _____

Schedule

:	
:	
:	
:	
:	
:	
:	
:	
:	
:	

Future Tasks

→
→
→
→

Tracker

? ? ? ? ? ? ? ? ? ?
? ? ? ? ? ? ? ? ? ?

DATE ....

Daily Planner

Daily Ta-Da's

1.
2.
3.

Check List

- _____
- _____
- _____
- _____
- _____
- _____
- _____
- _____
- _____

Schedule

:	
:	
:	
:	
:	
:	
:	
:	
:	
:	

Future Tasks

→
→
→
→

Tracker

(?)(?)(?)(?)(?)(?)(?)(?)(?)(?)
(?)(?)(?)(?)(?)(?)(?)(?)(?)(?)

DATE ....

DAILY PLANNER

DAILY TA-DA'S

1.
2.
3.

CHECK LIST

- _____
- _____
- _____
- _____
- _____
- _____
- _____
- _____
- _____
- _____

SCHEDULE

:	
:	
:	
:	
:	
:	
:	
:	
:	
:	

FUTURE TASKS

→
→
→
→

TRACKER

(?)(?)(?)(?)(?)(?)(?)(?)(?)(?)
(?)(?)(?)(?)(?)(?)(?)(?)(?)(?)

Sunday Review

On reflection, how did this week go?
_____
_____
_____
_____
_____
_____

What achievements am I proud of this week?
_____
_____
_____
_____
_____
_____

Who is the woman I need to become to achieve my goals?
_____
_____
_____
_____
_____
_____

Little promises I'm making to myself for next week
_____
_____
_____
_____
_____
_____

Notes

Notes

WEEK 02

A GREAT SYSTEM IS A SHORTCUT TO HAVING MORE TIME TO DO OTHER (FUN) STUFF

W/C ....

My Week's Appointments

Monday

Tuesday

Wednesday

Thursday

Friday

Saturday

Sunday

Notes:

MASTER TA-DA! LIST

Write down everything that NEEDS to get done this week.

....
....
....
....
....
....
....
....
....
....
....
....
....
....
....
....
....
....
....
....
....
....
....
....
....
....
....
....
....
....

Now, cross out everything off this list that doesn't belong to YOU. This is YOUR ta-da! list and is for YOUR important things this week.

DAILY TA-DA'S!

Write 4 things in each day, no more.

MONDAY
- ☐ ....
- ☐ ....
- ☐ ....
- ☐ ....

TUESDAY
- ☐ ....
- ☐ ....
- ☐ ....
- ☐ ....

WEDNESDAY
- ☐ ....
- ☐ ....
- ☐ ....
- ☐ ....

THURSDAY
- ☐ ....
- ☐ ....
- ☐ ....
- ☐ ....

FRIDAY
- ☐ ....
- ☐ ....
- ☐ ....
- ☐ ....

SATURDAY
- ☐ ....
- ☐ ....
- ☐ ....
- ☐ ....

SUNDAY
- ☐ ....
- ☐ ....
- ☐ ....
- ☐ ....

SOMETIME THIS WEEK
- ☐ ....
- ☐ ....
- ☐ ....
- ☐ ....

WEEKLY MEAL PLANNER

SUNDAY	
SATURDAY	
FRIDAY	
THURSDAY	
WEDNESDAY	
TUESDAY	
MONDAY	

Shopping List

Notes

WEEKLY FITNESS PLANNER

Progress & Focus

SUNDAY

SATURDAY

FRIDAY

THURSDAY

WEDNESDAY

TUESDAY

MONDAY

Notes

DATE ....

Daily Planner

Daily Ta-Da's

1.
2.
3.

Check List

- ☑ _____
- ☑ _____
- ☑ _____
- ☑ _____
- ☑ _____
- ☑ _____
- ☑ _____
- ☑ _____
- ☑ _____
- ☑ _____

Schedule

:	
:	
:	
:	
:	
:	
:	
:	
:	
:	

Future Tasks

→
→
→
→

Tracker

DATE ....

DAILY PLANNER

DAILY TA-DA'S

1.
2.
3.

CHECK LIST

- _____
- _____
- _____
- _____
- _____
- _____
- _____
- _____
- _____

SCHEDULE

:	
:	
:	
:	
:	
:	
:	
:	
:	
:	

FUTURE TASKS

→
→
→
→

TRACKER

DATE ....

Daily Planner

Daily Ta-Da's

1.
2.
3.

Check List

- _____
- _____
- _____
- _____
- _____
- _____
- _____
- _____
- _____
- _____

Schedule

:	
:	
:	
:	
:	
:	
:	
:	
:	
:	

Future Tasks

→
→
→
→

Tracker

? ? ? ? ? ? ? ? ? ?
? ? ? ? ? ? ? ? ? ?

Date ....

Daily Planner

Daily Ta-Da's

1.
2.
3.

Check List

Schedule

:	
:	
:	
:	
:	
:	
:	
:	
:	
:	

Future Tasks

→
→
→
→

Tracker

DATE ....

Daily Planner

Daily Ta-Da's

1.
2.
3.

Check List

- ☑ _____
- ☑ _____
- ☑ _____
- ☑ _____
- ☑ _____
- ☑ _____
- ☑ _____
- ☑ _____
- ☑ _____

Schedule

:	
:	
:	
:	
:	
:	
:	
:	
:	
:	

Future Tasks

→
→
→
→

Tracker

? ? ? ? ? ? ? ? ? ?
? ? ? ? ? ? ? ? ? ?

DATE ....

DAILY PLANNER

DAILY TA-DA'S

1.
2.
3.

CHECK LIST

- _____
- _____
- _____
- _____
- _____
- _____
- _____
- _____
- _____

SCHEDULE

:	
:	
:	
:	
:	
:	
:	
:	
:	
:	

FUTURE TASKS

→
→
→
→

TRACKER

(?)(?)(?)(?)(?)(?)(?)(?)(?)(?)
(?)(?)(?)(?)(?)(?)(?)(?)(?)(?)

DATE ....

DAILY PLANNER

DAILY TA-DA'S

1.
2.
3.

CHECK LIST

- _____
- _____
- _____
- _____
- _____
- _____
- _____
- _____
- _____
- _____

SCHEDULE

:	
:	
:	
:	
:	
:	
:	
:	
:	
:	

FUTURE TASKS

→
→
→
→

TRACKER

(?)(?)(?)(?)(?)(?)(?)(?)(?)(?)
(?)(?)(?)(?)(?)(?)(?)(?)(?)(?)

Sunday Review

On reflection, how did this week go?

What achievements am I proud of this week?

Who is the woman I need to become to achieve my goals?

Little promises I'm making to myself for next week

Notes

Notes

WEEK 03

GETTING ORGANISED IS A WHOLE
BUCKET FULL OF SELF LOVE & WORTH

WWW.KATEGROSVENOR.COM

W/C ....

My Week's Appointments

Monday	Tuesday	Wednesday

Thursday	Friday	Saturday
		Sunday

Notes:

MASTER TA-DA! LIST

WRITE DOWN EVERYTHING THAT NEEDS TO GET DONE THIS WEEK.

....
....
....
....
....
....
....
....
....
....
....
....
....
....
....
....
....
....
....
....
....
....
....
....
....
....
....
....
....
....
....
....

NOW, CROSS OUT EVERYTHING OFF THIS LIST THAT DOESN'T BELONG TO YOU.
THIS IS YOUR TA-DA! LIST AND IS FOR YOUR IMPORTANT THINGS THIS WEEK.

DAILY TA-DA'S!

Write 4 things in each day, no more.

MONDAY
- ☐ ....
- ☐ ....
- ☐ ....
- ☐ ....

TUESDAY
- ☐ ....
- ☐ ....
- ☐ ....
- ☐ ....

WEDNESDAY
- ☐ ....
- ☐ ....
- ☐ ....
- ☐ ....

THURSDAY
- ☐ ....
- ☐ ....
- ☐ ....
- ☐ ....

FRIDAY
- ☐ ....
- ☐ ....
- ☐ ....
- ☐ ....

SATURDAY
- ☐ ....
- ☐ ....
- ☐ ....
- ☐ ....

SUNDAY
- ☐ ....
- ☐ ....
- ☐ ....
- ☐ ....

SOMETIME THIS WEEK
- ☐ ....
- ☐ ....
- ☐ ....
- ☐ ....

WEEKLY MEAL PLANNER

SUNDAY	
SATURDAY	
FRIDAY	
THURSDAY	
WEDNESDAY	
TUESDAY	
MONDAY	

Shopping List

Notes

WEEKLY FITNESS PLANNER

Progress & Focus

Sunday

Saturday

Friday

Thursday

Wednesday

Tuesday

Monday

Notes

Date ....

Daily Planner

Daily Ta-Da's
1.
2.
3.

Check List
-
-
-
-
-
-
-
-
-
-

Schedule

:	
:	
:	
:	
:	
:	
:	
:	
:	
:	

Future Tasks
→
→
→
→

Tracker

DATE ....

DAILY PLANNER

DAILY TA-DA'S

1.
2.
3.

CHECK LIST

- ✓ _____
- ✓ _____
- ✓ _____
- ✓ _____
- ✓ _____
- ✓ _____
- ✓ _____
- ✓ _____
- ✓ _____
- ✓ _____

SCHEDULE

:	
:	
:	
:	
:	
:	
:	
:	
:	
:	

FUTURE TASKS

→
→
→
→

TRACKER

(?)(?)(?)(?)(?)(?)(?)(?)(?)(?)
(?)(?)(?)(?)(?)(?)(?)(?)(?)(?)

DATE ....

DAILY PLANNER

DAILY TA-DA'S

1.
2.
3.

CHECK LIST

SCHEDULE

:	
:	
:	
:	
:	
:	
:	
:	
:	
:	

FUTURE TASKS

→
→
→
→

TRACKER

DATE ....

Daily Planner

Daily Ta-Da's

1.
2.
3.

Check List

Schedule

:	
:	
:	
:	
:	
:	
:	
:	
:	
:	

Future Tasks

→
→
→
→

Tracker

DATE ....

DAILY PLANNER

DAILY TA-DA'S

1.
2.
3.

CHECK LIST

- _____
- _____
- _____
- _____
- _____
- _____
- _____
- _____
- _____
- _____

SCHEDULE

:	
:	
:	
:	
:	
:	
:	
:	
:	
:	

FUTURE TASKS

→
→
→
→

TRACKER

? ? ? ? ? ? ? ? ? ?
? ? ? ? ? ? ? ? ? ?

DATE ....

DAILY PLANNER

DAILY TA-DA'S

1.
2.
3.

CHECK LIST

- _____
- _____
- _____
- _____
- _____
- _____
- _____
- _____
- _____
- _____

SCHEDULE

:	
:	
:	
:	
:	
:	
:	
:	
:	
:	

FUTURE TASKS

→
→
→
→

TRACKER

(?)(?)(?)(?)(?)(?)(?)(?)(?)(?)
(?)(?)(?)(?)(?)(?)(?)(?)(?)(?)

Date ....

Daily Planner

Daily Ta-Da's

1.
2.
3.

Check List

-
-
-
-
-
-
-
-
-
-

Schedule

:	
:	
:	
:	
:	
:	
:	
:	
:	
:	

Future Tasks

→
→
→
→

Tracker

(?)(?)(?)(?)(?)(?)(?)(?)(?)(?)
(?)(?)(?)(?)(?)(?)(?)(?)(?)(?)

Sunday Review

On reflection, how did this week go?
_____
_____
_____
_____
_____
_____

What achievements am I proud of this week?
_____
_____
_____
_____
_____
_____

Who is the woman I need to become to achieve my goals?
_____
_____
_____
_____
_____

Little promises I'm making to myself for next week
_____
_____
_____
_____
_____
_____

Notes

Notes

WEEK 04

MESS AROUND US TRANSLATES TO CHAOS IN OUR MINDS

WWW.KATEGROSVENOR.COM

W/C ....

My Week's Appointments

Monday	Tuesday	Wednesday

Thursday	Friday	Saturday
		Sunday

Notes:

MASTER TA-DA! LIST

Write down everything that needs to get done this week.

....
....
....
....
....
....
....
....
....
....
....
....
....
....
....
....
....
....
....
....
....
....
....
....
....
....
....
....
....
....
....
....

Now, cross out everything off this list that doesn't belong to YOU.
This is YOUR ta-da! list and is for YOUR important things this week.

DAILY TA-DA'S!

Write 4 things in each day, no more.

MONDAY
- ☐ ....
- ☐ ....
- ☐ ....
- ☐ ....

TUESDAY
- ☐ ....
- ☐ ....
- ☐ ....
- ☐ ....

WEDNESDAY
- ☐ ....
- ☐ ....
- ☐ ....
- ☐ ....

THURSDAY
- ☐ ....
- ☐ ....
- ☐ ....
- ☐ ....

FRIDAY
- ☐ ....
- ☐ ....
- ☐ ....
- ☐ ....

SATURDAY
- ☐ ....
- ☐ ....
- ☐ ....
- ☐ ....

SUNDAY
- ☐ ....
- ☐ ....
- ☐ ....
- ☐ ....

SOMETIME THIS WEEK
- ☐ ....
- ☐ ....
- ☐ ....
- ☐ ....

WEEKLY MEAL PLANNER

SUNDAY

SATURDAY

FRIDAY

THURSDAY

WEDNESDAY

TUESDAY

MONDAY

SHOPPING LIST

NOTES

WEEKLY FITNESS PLANNER

PROGRESS & FOCUS

SUNDAY	
SATURDAY	
FRIDAY	
THURSDAY	
WEDNESDAY	
TUESDAY	
MONDAY	

NOTES

DATE ....

Daily Planner

Daily Ta-Da's

1.
2.
3.

Check List

- [ ] _____
- [ ] _____
- [ ] _____
- [ ] _____
- [ ] _____
- [ ] _____
- [ ] _____
- [ ] _____
- [ ] _____

Schedule

:	
:	
:	
:	
:	
:	
:	
:	
:	
:	

Future Tasks

→
→
→
→

Tracker

(?)(?)(?)(?)(?)(?)(?)(?)(?)(?)
(?)(?)(?)(?)(?)(?)(?)(?)(?)(?)

DATE ....

DAILY PLANNER

DAILY TA-DA'S

1.
2.
3.

CHECK LIST

- [ ]
- [ ]
- [ ]
- [ ]
- [ ]
- [ ]
- [ ]
- [ ]
- [ ]
- [ ]

SCHEDULE

:	
:	
:	
:	
:	
:	
:	
:	
:	
:	

FUTURE TASKS

→
→
→
→

TRACKER

(?)(?)(?)(?)(?)(?)(?)(?)(?)(?)
(?)(?)(?)(?)(?)(?)(?)(?)(?)(?)

DATE ....

DAILY PLANNER

DAILY TA-DA'S

1.
2.
3.

CHECK LIST

- [ ] _____
- [ ] _____
- [ ] _____
- [ ] _____
- [ ] _____
- [ ] _____
- [ ] _____
- [ ] _____
- [ ] _____

SCHEDULE

:	
:	
:	
:	
:	
:	
:	
:	
:	
:	

FUTURE TASKS

→
→
→
→

TRACKER

(?)(?)(?)(?)(?)(?)(?)(?)(?)(?)
(?)(?)(?)(?)(?)(?)(?)(?)(?)(?)

DATE ....

Daily Planner

Daily Ta-Da's

1.
2.
3.

Check List

- _____
- _____
- _____
- _____
- _____
- _____
- _____
- _____
- _____
- _____

Schedule

:	
:	
:	
:	
:	
:	
:	
:	
:	
:	

Future Tasks

→
→
→
→

Tracker

(?)(?)(?)(?)(?)(?)(?)(?)(?)(?)
(?)(?)(?)(?)(?)(?)(?)(?)(?)(?)

DATE ....

Daily Planner

Daily Ta-Da's

1.
2.
3.

Check List

-
-
-
-
-
-
-
-
-
-

Schedule

:	
:	
:	
:	
:	
:	
:	
:	
:	
:	

Future Tasks

→
→
→
→

Tracker

(?)(?)(?)(?)(?)(?)(?)(?)(?)(?)
(?)(?)(?)(?)(?)(?)(?)(?)(?)(?)

Date ....

Daily Planner

Daily Ta-Da's

1.
2.
3.

Check List

Schedule

:	
:	
:	
:	
:	
:	
:	
:	
:	
:	

Future Tasks

→
→
→
→

Tracker

Date ....

Daily Planner

Daily Ta-Da's

1.
2.
3.

Check List

- ☑ _____
- ☑ _____
- ☑ _____
- ☑ _____
- ☑ _____
- ☑ _____
- ☑ _____
- ☑ _____
- ☑ _____

Schedule

:	
:	
:	
:	
:	
:	
:	
:	
:	
:	

Future Tasks

→ _____
→ _____
→ _____
→ _____

Tracker

(?)(?)(?)(?)(?)(?)(?)(?)(?)(?)
(?)(?)(?)(?)(?)(?)(?)(?)(?)(?)

Sunday Review

On reflection, how did this week go?

_____
_____
_____
_____
_____
_____

What achievements am I proud of this week?

_____
_____
_____
_____
_____
_____

Who is the woman I need to become to achieve my goals?

_____
_____
_____
_____
_____
_____

Little promises I'm making to myself for next week

_____
_____
_____
_____
_____
_____

Notes

Notes

Month 03

A PLACE FOR EVERYTHING, AND
EVERYTHING IN ITS PLACE

MRS BEETON

WWW.KATEGROSVENOR.COM

My Month at a Glance

S	M	T	W	Th	F	S

Notes:

Goal Setting
Reflecting and Looking Ahead

Top Moments ★	Most Proud of ★	Promises to Make Myself ★

Personal Goals	9-5 Goals	Health Goals

I will Try to Stop	I would Like To Learn	Habits I want to Adopt

People I want to Connect with	I want to Save	I want to Buy

Goal Tracker
Pick Your Top 3 Goals for this Month

GOAL: _____

START DATE: _____

DEADLINE: _____

Break down goals into daily action steps.
Track progress below.

Date	Task	Description	Deadline	Status

Monthly Project Planning

Reflection

What was working	What was not working

Get Busy & Source

Project To-Do List	Project Supply List

Schedule It!

Sunday	Monday	Tuesday	Wednesday	Thursday	Friday	Saturday

Monthly Expenses

RECURRING EXPENSES

Memberships, etc.	Amount
TOTAL RECURRING EXPENSES	£

VARIABLE EXPENSES

	Amount
TOTAL VARIABLE EXPENSES	£
TOTAL MONTHLY EXPENSES	£

Monthly Cleaning Plan

Sunday	Monday	Tuesday	Wednesday	Thursday	Friday	Saturday	Sunday

Daily
- [ ]
- [ ]
- [ ]
- [ ]

Weekly
- [ ]
- [ ]
- [ ]
- [ ]

Monthly
- [ ]
- [ ]
- [ ]
- [ ]

Monthly Decluttering Plan

KITCHEN

- Empty boxes of food
- Expired food
- Chipped/cracked dishes, plates, etc.
- Bent cutlery
- Rusty/dull knives
- Stained/broken/worn kitchen utensils
- Tidy plastic bags, ties, and clips
- Sort Tupperware - bin any with missing lids
- Bin and pans with cracked/peeling non-stick
- Clean and fill condiment jars/spices
- Wash oven gloves, etc. and restock cloths
- Consolidate all cleaning products
- Wash and sanitise kitchen bin

BEDROOM

- Clean dressing table
- Wash make up brushes
- Bin any out-of-date/broken make up
- Remove old magazines/old books
- Clean shoes & bags and stuff with tissue paper
- Sell/send to charity shop any clothes that don't fit
- Recycle any torn clothes
- Remove any clothes out of season and store
- Sort socks. Bin any without pairs
- Bin any torn/stretched underwear
- Sort drawers and arrange according to use/colour

BATHROOM

- Clean under sink
- Bin old toothbrush/es
- Empty shampoo/conditioner
- Bin stretched hair ties
- Remove any tatty faceclothes/towels
- Throw away empty toiletries
- Bin dried up nail polish
- Restock cotton wool pads & buds
- Check sanitary products and consolidate
- Refill liquid soap

LAUNDRY

- Empty lint from tumble dryer
- Wash out detergent drawer
- Clean/sanitise washing machine
- Refil detergent/softener containers

CLEANING

- Recycle broken spray bottles
- Clean under sink and sanitise
- Consolidate all cleaning products
- Store excess brushes or sponges

NOTES

Notes

WEEK 01

YOU CAN BE LAZIER IF YOU'RE ORGANISED

(YOU DON'T HAVE TO SPEND TIME LOOKING FOR STUFF)

WWW.KATEGROSVENOR.COM

W/C ....

My Week's Appointments

Monday	Tuesday	Wednesday

Thursday	Friday	Saturday
		Sunday

Notes:

MASTER TA-DA! LIST

WRITE DOWN EVERYTHING THAT NEEDS TO GET DONE THIS WEEK.

....
....
....
....
....
....
....
....
....
....
....
....
....
....
....
....
....
....
....
....
....
....
....
....
....
....
....
....
....
....
....
....

NOW, CROSS OUT EVERYTHING OFF THIS LIST THAT DOESN'T BELONG TO YOU.
THIS IS YOUR TA-DA! LIST AND IS FOR YOUR IMPORTANT THINGS THIS WEEK.

DAILY TA-DA'S!

Write 4 things in each day, no more.

MONDAY
- ☐ ....
- ☐ ....
- ☐ ....
- ☐ ....

TUESDAY
- ☐ ....
- ☐ ....
- ☐ ....
- ☐ ....

WEDNESDAY
- ☐ ....
- ☐ ....
- ☐ ....
- ☐ ....

THURSDAY
- ☐ ....
- ☐ ....
- ☐ ....
- ☐ ....

FRIDAY
- ☐ ....
- ☐ ....
- ☐ ....
- ☐ ....

SATURDAY
- ☐ ....
- ☐ ....
- ☐ ....
- ☐ ....

SUNDAY
- ☐ ....
- ☐ ....
- ☐ ....
- ☐ ....

SOMETIME THIS WEEK
- ☐ ....
- ☐ ....
- ☐ ....
- ☐ ....

WEEKLY MEAL PLANNER

SUNDAY

SATURDAY

FRIDAY

THURSDAY

WEDNESDAY

TUESDAY

MONDAY

Shopping List

Notes

WEEKLY FITNESS PLANNER

Progress & Focus

Sunday

Saturday

Friday

Thursday

Wednesday

Tuesday

Monday

Notes

Date ....

Daily Planner

Daily Ta-Da's

1.
2.
3.

Check List

- [ ]
- [ ]
- [ ]
- [ ]
- [ ]
- [ ]
- [ ]
- [ ]
- [ ]

Schedule

:	
:	
:	
:	
:	
:	
:	
:	
:	
:	

Future Tasks

→
→
→
→

Tracker

? ? ? ? ? ? ? ? ? ?
? ? ? ? ? ? ? ? ? ?

DATE ....

DAILY PLANNER

DAILY TA-DA'S

1.
2.
3.

CHECK LIST

- _____
- _____
- _____
- _____
- _____
- _____
- _____
- _____
- _____
- _____

SCHEDULE

:	
:	
:	
:	
:	
:	
:	
:	
:	
:	

FUTURE TASKS

→
→
→
→

TRACKER

? ? ? ? ? ? ? ? ? ? ? ?
? ? ? ? ? ? ? ? ? ? ? ?

Date ....

Daily Planner

Daily Ta-Da's

1.
2.
3.

Check List

-
-
-
-
-
-
-
-
-
-

Schedule

:	
:	
:	
:	
:	
:	
:	
:	
:	
:	

Future Tasks

→
→
→
→

Tracker

Date ....

Daily Planner

Daily Ta-Da's

1.
2.
3.

Check List

- _____
- _____
- _____
- _____
- _____
- _____
- _____
- _____
- _____
- _____

Schedule

:	
:	
:	
:	
:	
:	
:	
:	
:	
:	

Future Tasks

→
→
→
→

Tracker

(?) (?) (?) (?) (?) (?) (?) (?) (?) (?)
(?) (?) (?) (?) (?) (?) (?) (?) (?) (?)

Date ....

Daily Planner

Daily Ta-Da's

1.
2.
3.

Check List

- [ ] _____
- [ ] _____
- [ ] _____
- [ ] _____
- [ ] _____
- [ ] _____
- [ ] _____
- [ ] _____
- [ ] _____
- [ ] _____

Schedule

:	
:	
:	
:	
:	
:	
:	
:	
:	
:	

Future Tasks

→
→
→
→

Tracker

(?)(?)(?)(?)(?)(?)(?)(?)(?)(?)
(?)(?)(?)(?)(?)(?)(?)(?)(?)(?)

DATE ....

Daily Planner

Daily Ta-Da's

1.
2.
3.

Check List

Schedule

Future Tasks

Tracker

DATE ....

Daily Planner

Daily Ta-Da's

1.
2.
3.

Check List

- _____
- _____
- _____
- _____
- _____
- _____
- _____
- _____
- _____

Schedule

:	
:	
:	
:	
:	
:	
:	
:	
:	
:	

Future Tasks

→
→
→
→

Tracker

? ? ? ? ? ? ? ? ? ?
? ? ? ? ? ? ? ? ? ?

Sunday Review

On reflection, how did this week go?

What achievements am I proud of this week?

Who is the woman I need to become to achieve my goals?

Little promises I'm making to myself for next week

Notes

NOTES

WEEK 02

"ORGANISING IS WHAT YOU DO BEFORE YOU DO SOMETHING, SO THAT WHEN YOU DO IT, IT IS NOT ALL MIXED UP."

A. A. MILNE

W/C ....

My Week's Appointments

Monday	Tuesday	Wednesday

Thursday	Friday	Saturday
		Sunday

Notes:

MASTER TA-DA! LIST

Write down everything that NEEDS to get done this week.

....
....
....
....
....
....
....
....
....
....
....
....
....
....
....
....
....
....
....
....
....
....
....
....
....
....
....
....
....
....
....
....
....

Now, cross out everything off this list that doesn't belong to YOU.
This is YOUR ta-da! list and is for YOUR important things this week.

DAILY TA-DA'S!

Write 4 things in each day, no more.

MONDAY
- ☐ ....
- ☐ ....
- ☐ ....
- ☐ ....

TUESDAY
- ☐ ....
- ☐ ....
- ☐ ....
- ☐ ....

WEDNESDAY
- ☐ ....
- ☐ ....
- ☐ ....
- ☐ ....

THURSDAY
- ☐ ....
- ☐ ....
- ☐ ....
- ☐ ....

FRIDAY
- ☐ ....
- ☐ ....
- ☐ ....
- ☐ ....

SATURDAY
- ☐ ....
- ☐ ....
- ☐ ....
- ☐ ....

SUNDAY
- ☐ ....
- ☐ ....
- ☐ ....
- ☐ ....

SOMETIME THIS WEEK
- ☐ ....
- ☐ ....
- ☐ ....
- ☐ ....

WEEKLY MEAL PLANNER

SUNDAY	
SATURDAY	
FRIDAY	
THURSDAY	
WEDNESDAY	
TUESDAY	
MONDAY	

Shopping List

Notes

WEEKLY FITNESS PLANNER

SUNDAY	**PROGRESS & FOCUS**
SATURDAY	
FRIDAY	
THURSDAY	
WEDNESDAY	
TUESDAY	
MONDAY	

NOTES

DATE ....

DAILY PLANNER

DAILY TA-DA'S

1.
2.
3.

CHECK LIST

- _____
- _____
- _____
- _____
- _____
- _____
- _____
- _____
- _____
- _____

SCHEDULE

:	
:	
:	
:	
:	
:	
:	
:	
:	
:	

FUTURE TASKS

→
→
→
→

TRACKER

(?)(?)(?)(?)(?)(?)(?)(?)(?)(?)
(?)(?)(?)(?)(?)(?)(?)(?)(?)(?)

DATE ....

Daily Planner

Daily Ta-Da's

1.
2.
3.

Check List

- _____
- _____
- _____
- _____
- _____
- _____
- _____
- _____
- _____
- _____

Schedule

:	
:	
:	
:	
:	
:	
:	
:	
:	
:	

Future Tasks

→
→
→
→

Tracker

DATE ....

DAILY PLANNER

DAILY TA-DA'S

1.
2.
3.

CHECK LIST

- [ ] _____
- [ ] _____
- [ ] _____
- [ ] _____
- [ ] _____
- [ ] _____
- [ ] _____
- [ ] _____
- [ ] _____
- [ ] _____

SCHEDULE

:	
:	
:	
:	
:	
:	
:	
:	
:	
:	

FUTURE TASKS

→
→
→
→

TRACKER

(?)(?)(?)(?)(?)(?)(?)(?)(?)(?)
(?)(?)(?)(?)(?)(?)(?)(?)(?)(?)

Date ....

Daily Planner

Daily Ta-Da's

1.
2.
3.

Check List

-
-
-
-
-
-
-
-
-
-

Schedule

:	
:	
:	
:	
:	
:	
:	
:	
:	
:	

Future Tasks

→
→
→
→

Tracker

(?)(?)(?)(?)(?)(?)(?)(?)(?)(?)(?)
(?)(?)(?)(?)(?)(?)(?)(?)(?)(?)(?)

DATE ....

Daily Planner

Daily Ta-Da's

1.
2.
3.

Check List

-
-
-
-
-
-
-
-
-
-

Schedule

:	
:	
:	
:	
:	
:	
:	
:	
:	
:	

Future Tasks

→
→
→
→

Tracker

DATE ....

Daily Planner

Daily Ta-Da's

1.
2.
3.

Check List

- _____
- _____
- _____
- _____
- _____
- _____
- _____
- _____
- _____
- _____

Schedule

:	
:	
:	
:	
:	
:	
:	
:	
:	
:	

Future Tasks

→
→
→
→

Tracker

DATE ....

Daily Planner

Daily Ta-Da's

1.
2.
3.

Check List

-
-
-
-
-
-
-
-
-
-

Schedule

:	
:	
:	
:	
:	
:	
:	
:	
:	
:	

Future Tasks

→
→
→
→

Tracker

(?)(?)(?)(?)(?)(?)(?)(?)(?)(?)
(?)(?)(?)(?)(?)(?)(?)(?)(?)(?)

Sunday Review

On reflection, how did this week go?

What achievements am I proud of this week?

Who is the woman I need to become to achieve my goals?

Little promises I'm making to myself for next week

NOTES

Notes

WEEK 03

THE DIFFERENCE BETWEEN BEING DISORGANISED AND ORGANISED IS JUST OUR DAILY HABITS.

WWW.KATEGROSVENOR.COM

W/C ....

My Week's Appointments

Monday	Tuesday	Wednesday

Thursday	Friday	Saturday
		Sunday

Notes:

MASTER TA-DA! LIST

WRITE DOWN EVERYTHING THAT NEEDS TO GET DONE THIS WEEK.

....
....
....
....
....
....
....
....
....
....
....
....
....
....
....
....
....
....
....
....
....
....
....
....
....
....
....
....
....
....
....
....
....

NOW, CROSS OUT EVERYTHING OFF THIS LIST THAT DOESN'T BELONG TO YOU.
THIS IS YOUR TA-DA! LIST AND IS FOR YOUR IMPORTANT THINGS THIS WEEK.

DAILY TA-DA'S!

Write 4 things in each day, no more.

MONDAY	TUESDAY
☐	☐ ....
☐	☐ ....
☐	☐ ....
☐	☐ ....

WEDNESDAY	THURSDAY
☐	☐ ....
☐	☐ ....
☐	☐ ....
☐	☐ ....

FRIDAY	SATURDAY
☐	☐ ....
☐	☐ ....
☐	☐ ....
☐	☐ ....

SUNDAY	SOMETIME THIS WEEK
☐	☐ ....
☐	☐ ....
☐	☐ ....
☐	☐ ....

WEEKLY MEAL PLANNER

SUNDAY

SATURDAY

FRIDAY

THURSDAY

WEDNESDAY

TUESDAY

MONDAY

Shopping List

Notes

WEEKLY FITNESS PLANNER

SUNDAY

SATURDAY

FRIDAY

THURSDAY

WEDNESDAY

TUESDAY

MONDAY

Progress & Focus

Notes

DATE ....

DAILY PLANNER

DAILY TA-DA'S

1.
2.
3.

CHECK LIST

- _____
- _____
- _____
- _____
- _____
- _____
- _____
- _____
- _____
- _____

SCHEDULE

:	
:	
:	
:	
:	
:	
:	
:	
:	
:	

FUTURE TASKS

→
→
→
→

TRACKER

(?)(?)(?)(?)(?)(?)(?)(?)(?)(?)
(?)(?)(?)(?)(?)(?)(?)(?)(?)(?)

DATE ....

DAILY PLANNER

DAILY TA-DA'S

1.
2.
3.

CHECK LIST

- _____
- _____
- _____
- _____
- _____
- _____
- _____
- _____
- _____
- _____

SCHEDULE

:	
:	
:	
:	
:	
:	
:	
:	
:	
:	

FUTURE TASKS

→
→
→
→

TRACKER

(?)(?)(?)(?)(?)(?)(?)(?)(?)(?)
(?)(?)(?)(?)(?)(?)(?)(?)(?)(?)

DATE ....

DAILY PLANNER

DAILY TA-DA'S

1.
2.
3.

CHECK LIST

- _____
- _____
- _____
- _____
- _____
- _____
- _____
- _____
- _____

SCHEDULE

:	
:	
:	
:	
:	
:	
:	
:	
:	
:	

FUTURE TASKS

→
→
→
→

TRACKER

DATE ....

Daily Planner

Daily Ta-Da's

1.
2.
3.

Check List

Schedule

Future Tasks

Tracker

DATE ....

Daily Planner

Daily Ta-Da's

1.
2.
3.

Check List

Schedule

Future Tasks

Tracker

DATE ....

DAILY PLANNER

DAILY TA-DA'S

1.
2.
3.

CHECK LIST

- _____
- _____
- _____
- _____
- _____
- _____
- _____
- _____
- _____
- _____

SCHEDULE

:	
:	
:	
:	
:	
:	
:	
:	
:	
:	

FUTURE TASKS

→
→
→
→

TRACKER

DATE ....

Daily Planner

Daily Ta-Da's

1.
2.
3.

Check List

- [ ] _____
- [ ] _____
- [ ] _____
- [ ] _____
- [ ] _____
- [ ] _____
- [ ] _____
- [ ] _____
- [ ] _____

Schedule

:	
:	
:	
:	
:	
:	
:	
:	
:	
:	

Future Tasks

→
→
→
→

Tracker

(?)(?)(?)(?)(?)(?)(?)(?)(?)(?)
(?)(?)(?)(?)(?)(?)(?)(?)(?)(?)

Sunday Review

On reflection, how did this week go?

_____
_____
_____
_____
_____
_____

What achievements am I proud of this week?

_____
_____
_____
_____
_____
_____

Who is the woman I need to become to achieve my goals?

_____
_____
_____
_____
_____
_____

Little promises I'm making to myself for next week

_____
_____
_____
_____
_____
_____

NOTES

Notes

WEEK 04

ORGANISING IS A JOURNEY,
NOT A DESTINATION.

WWW.KATEGROSVENOR.COM

W/C ....

My Week's Appointments

Monday	Tuesday	Wednesday

Thursday	Friday	Saturday
		Sunday

Notes:

MASTER TA-DA! LIST

Write down everything that NEEDS to get done this week.

....
....
....
....
....
....
....
....
....
....
....
....
....
....
....
....
....
....
....
....
....
....
....
....
....
....
....
....
....
....
....
....
....
....

Now, cross out everything off this list that doesn't belong to YOU.
This is YOUR ta-da! list and is for YOUR important things this week.

DAILY TA-DA'S!

Write 4 things in each day, no more.

MONDAY	TUESDAY
☐	☐ ....
☐	☐ ....
☐	☐ ....
☐	☐ ....

WEDNESDAY	THURSDAY
☐	☐ ....
☐	☐ ....
☐	☐ ....
☐	☐ ....

FRIDAY	SATURDAY
☐	☐ ....
☐	☐ ....
☐	☐ ....
☐	☐ ....

SUNDAY	SOMETIME THIS WEEK
☐	☐ ....
☐	☐ ....
☐	☐ ....
☐	☐ ....

WEEKLY MEAL PLANNER

SUNDAY	
SATURDAY	
FRIDAY	
THURSDAY	
WEDNESDAY	
TUESDAY	
MONDAY	

SHOPPING LIST

NOTES

WEEKLY FITNESS PLANNER

SUNDAY	PROGRESS & FOCUS
SATURDAY	
FRIDAY	
THURSDAY	
WEDNESDAY	
TUESDAY	
MONDAY	

NOTES

DATE ....

Daily Planner

Daily Ta-Da's

1.
2.
3.

Check List

- [ ] _____
- [ ] _____
- [ ] _____
- [ ] _____
- [ ] _____
- [ ] _____
- [ ] _____
- [ ] _____
- [ ] _____
- [ ] _____

Schedule

:	
:	
:	
:	
:	
:	
:	
:	
:	
:	

Future Tasks

→
→
→
→

Tracker

(?)(?)(?)(?)(?)(?)(?)(?)(?)(?)
(?)(?)(?)(?)(?)(?)(?)(?)(?)(?)

DATE ....

Daily Planner

Daily Ta-Da's

1.
2.
3.

Check List

- _____
- _____
- _____
- _____
- _____
- _____
- _____
- _____
- _____

Schedule

:	
:	
:	
:	
:	
:	
:	
:	
:	
:	

Future Tasks

→
→
→
→

Tracker

(?)(?)(?)(?)(?)(?)(?)(?)(?)(?)
(?)(?)(?)(?)(?)(?)(?)(?)(?)(?)

DATE ....

Daily Planner

Daily Ta-Da's

1.
2.
3.

Check List

- _____
- _____
- _____
- _____
- _____
- _____
- _____
- _____
- _____
- _____

Schedule

:	
:	
:	
:	
:	
:	
:	
:	
:	
:	

Future Tasks

→
→
→
→

Tracker

? ? ? ? ? ? ? ? ? ?
? ? ? ? ? ? ? ? ? ?

Date ....

Daily Planner

Daily Ta-Da's

1.
2.
3.

Check List

Schedule

Future Tasks

Tracker

DATE ....

Daily Planner

Daily Ta-Da's

1.
2.
3.

Check List

- _____
- _____
- _____
- _____
- _____
- _____
- _____
- _____
- _____
- _____

Schedule

:	
:	
:	
:	
:	
:	
:	
:	
:	
:	

Future Tasks

→
→
→
→

Tracker

? ? ? ? ? ? ? ? ? ?
? ? ? ? ? ? ? ? ? ?

DATE ....

Daily Planner

Daily Ta-Da's

1.
2.
3.

Check List

Schedule

:	
:	
:	
:	
:	
:	
:	
:	
:	
:	

Future Tasks

→
→
→
→

Tracker

Date ....

Daily Planner

Daily Ta-Da's

1.
2.
3.

Check List

-
-
-
-
-
-
-
-
-

Schedule

:	
:	
:	
:	
:	
:	
:	
:	
:	
:	

Future Tasks

→
→
→
→

Tracker

? ? ? ? ? ? ? ? ? ?
? ? ? ? ? ? ? ? ? ?

Sunday Review

On reflection, how did this week go?

_____
_____
_____
_____
_____
_____

What achievements am I proud of this week?

_____
_____
_____
_____
_____
_____

Who is the woman I need to become to achieve my goals?

_____
_____
_____
_____
_____

Little promises I'm making to myself for next week

_____
_____
_____
_____
_____
_____

Notes

Notes

Notes

Notes

Notes

Notes

Notes

Notes

Notes

Notes

Notes

Notes

Notes

Notes

Notes

NOTES

Notes

Notes

Notes

Notes

Notes

Notes

Notes

NOTES

Notes

Notes

Notes

Printed in Great Britain
by Amazon